Lanterns in the Sky
& other poems

KEYA JADHAV

First published in 2021 by
BecomeShakespeare.com

One Point Six Technologies Pvt Ltd.
119-123, 1st Floor, Building J2, B - Wing, WadalaTruck Terminal,
Wadala East, Mumbai, Maharashtra, India, 400022.
T:+91 8080226699

ISBN: 978-93-5458-770-2

I dedicate this book to the fragile dreams of many others like me.

ACKNOWLEDGEMENTS

I'm grateful to my family and extended family, my mother Deepa and younger sister Ira who supported me to publish my work, and my father Uday Jadhav who introduced me to a world beyond my school books; the first person to read, admire and criticize my writings. I sincerely thank my English teacher Mrs. Usha Krishnan who fueled my interest in literature during the freshman year of high school. I am fortunate that I had helping hands of Mansi Ghadge, Ahana Dutta and Maya Sodder to fill my book with such beautiful and life-like illustrations. I would also like to take this opportunity to express my heartfelt gratitude to Suman and Raghu Beedu.

FOREWORD

George Bernard Shaw once said, "What we want is to see the child in pursuit of knowledge, and not knowledge in pursuit of the child." And, as her teacher, that is exactly what I see in Keya. She poured all her talent into her writing, beginning with a daily journal and then progressively transforming her thoughts and ideas into poems. Keya is a voracious reader and this has helped her unleash her imagination. Though inspired by poets like Longfellow, Robert Frost, Walter Frost and Sylvia Plath, her writing is uniquely her own – drawn from her everyday life and the people around her, from situations and things that fascinate her.

If surrealism seeks to examine the unconscious realm by means of the written word, to stretch language to its limits to transform it into an instrument for exploring the human psyche, then Keya's poems are undoubtedly surrealistic. At the same time, her poetry is thought-provoking and encourages serious introspection adding more than a dash of realism. The imagery she brings to her poetry, juxtaposing the mundane with the imaginary, results in a delightful blend that surprises the senses.

In the grand scheme of things, it is not only our action but also our inaction that defines us. Keya delves into how and why of our doubting mind paralyses us into inaction. In a world filled with fear – resulting from the pandemic, from losing a loved one, from the uncertainty in our lives-her poems bring us hope. Hope found in the rising sun, a soft feather, a singing bird. There are lighter moments too - worth more than a chuckle. I couldn't stop laughing after reading The Lone Bird.

As someone who teaches English, I am fascinated by the way she uses imagery, similes and metaphors in her poems. Her poems are predominantly 'language poetry', eschewing theory-driven conversations, in favor of a more compelling narrative. Far from being maudlin, the poems create an atmosphere charged with positivity that end with the hope of finding one's true self. Keya's poetry is the "true confession of a life learned lesson".

Usha Krishnan

M.A (English), B.Ed.

Delhi Public School

ABOUT THE AUTHOR

Keya Uday Jadhav was born in Mumbai in 2004 and studied at Delhi Public School Navi Mumbai. She has penned down her thoughts on paper and created poetry out of them in her high school years. One of her hobbies include reading, from where she got her inspiration to write. She is specifically interested in learning about poetry, proses and sonnets. She hasn't found her muse yet, so her journey from writing in a diary to publishing a book has come a long way by finding beauty in ordinary, small things or the desire to imbibe oneself in it. This book is her first publication and includes a variety of poems and proses.

CONTENTS

OLD MAN LAUGHING.......

Old man laughing at the end of the street
His smile widens as his eyes grow weak
He has nothing to lose and nothing to eat
Yet he calmly continues to speak

Old man laughing at the end of the street
At the people passing by
With their fast-moving feet
And hear them sigh
As they glare at him
Ignorant of his experience
In a world so grim

Old man laughing at the end of the street
Recollecting his youth
And the misery associated with it
His wife lies in a cemetery
His children drifted away
So he appears to be wary
But still chuckles the whole day

Old man laughing at the end of the street
He is suffering from a syndrome
His death he can't beat
His value is depreciated
In the eyes of the society
But he doesn't mind being hated
For it's time to unite with the deity

Old man laughing at the end of the street
No funeral home to resist
When his heart doesn't beat
And his smile ceases to exist

A LONE BIRD

A lone bird chirping
Sitting on a barbed wire
Hearing men sing
As they start the forest fire

No companion with him
No worms in sight
Can't function with his whim
So to be angered is right

He plans his revenge finally
Another shirt would cost a buck
They swear initially
But then consider it good luck

A creature so small
Can only waive the white flag
Or join his friends in the fall
To a new land and sag

Yet he continues to stay
On the line of death
An undeserved price to pay
Like the victims of Macbeth

Years bring back
Almost the same things burned
But comes again an attack
Of mankind unconcerned

SUMMER POEM

A blissful noon
Spent sitting in the lawn
You can tell it's June
When the leaves are no more fawn

The air carries a toxic sweetness
Caused by a margarita
It only fuels my happiness
With a lightly grilled pita

The tickling feeling in my feet
Momentarily shifts to present
Despite the heat
I relish the moment

The sprinkler which spins
Soaks my cotton dress
The penetration into my skin begins
A healing process

Losing my vice
Gulping from a glass
I keep adding cubes of ice
As a cool breeze tries to trespass

I put on some music
The trees listen too
A calm dance they pick
That we both do

A few hours just fly by
As I switch to lemonade
A girl once so shy
Her timidness seems to fade

The sun towards the west hurled
The glass reflecting one last ray
Little drop of the green world
Enough to chase the summer away

A FEATHER

A feather levitates

Out of the dustpan

Which the maid used

To sweep the house clean

Out of the casement

The wind is its vehicle

Giving it a free ride

Making it feel like "the feather"

Trusting the wind with its soft body

To see the whole world

Floating like a piece of paper

Free from human possession

The different coloured trees

Are enormous and overwhelming

It shamelessly exposes itself

To the hammock of leaves

Up on the top of a hill

Watching humans move like ants

They have shrunken to its size

Yet their needs tend to stay the same

"A trap is a requisite for success in life"

Says the wind to a feather

As they go hand in hand to their next destination

A land of surprises awaits to come

The wind carries it to paradise on earth

Where is paradise after life?

It doesn't mind the same air carrying million others

Why do we fight the wind then?

Isn't it just one power that helps?

No pictures, no words can express the beauty

Of what a feather sees

Celebrating its dispensable life

As it floats away

The rain that weighs it down

Pours to glisten this earth

It finds warmth in a new room

Only to end up on the floor

Lying beside is another feather

Oblivious to this journey

Keya Jadhav

TONIGHT

Have we seen the beautiful, starry night?

The slow changes that take place

A dream-like reality we leave behind when we sleep

This slumber prevents us from entering a world of wonders, one that a man hasn't ever witnessed properly

Stars marking the sky like moles on our body

Mosquitoes crowding under the street light like cars on the highway

Children out to play in the evening are preparing for bedtime

Shadows guarding what we consider "precious"

We conceded the value of that

All I can look at is the black sky

What makes it so soothing?

I never knew empty space could fill me with emotions

What grief evokes a deep thought in me?

A fleeting contemplation makes me still

Time paints the twilight

Every celestial body is busy,

The sun prepares me to look the world in the face

The moon being the gateway to a world of sin

I look out the window, high up, while the darkness settles on the garden below

I can barely make out the shapes of the plants

It gives me comfort as the others sleep soundly
My little hands are covered by the sleeves of my sweater
I draw the curtains slowly, as if someone is going to notice me
The houses look empty
Liveliness has disappeared
I have my eyes, my ears, and my lips to myself
Looking into the distance, I hear the fan spin
The slow breeze outside the window overpowers the whir
I wish to be on the unknown side,
Where I can perceive things beyond my projection
Where I can see the worth of festive crickets
Where I can feel the tranquillity of the chilly wind
Where I can hear the probability of a shooting star
Till I fall asleep.

Keya Jadhav

THE LAST DATE

Today morning you texted me

Asking me to meet you near the cafe

I put on the blue dress for you

Imagining you in a white shirt, as always

I walk down this endless road

Which brings me to you

A bicycle date is what you plan

Oh! You know me so well

Something flutters in me

Is it my conscious heart?

We're sitting on the bicycle

You calmly drive it

The picnic mat is my magic carpet

But my feelings run parallel

You lay your head on my lap

Why today?

Professing love sustained us

You enquire about my life

Like you did yesterday

You unpack the lunch parcel

I put up my hair

Quickly stealing a glance
You proceed with eating
Finally you embrace my passion
We've loved to become one
Tremendous courage flows to you
"Can we not be formal?"
I'm the one you sold your fear to
I smile to our confrontation
Don't need to find the "true" now
You drop me home as it gets late
An awkward silence between us
Yet our eyes continue to meet
I watch you leave, as you walk your bike
That was the last time I saw you………

Keya Jadhav

LANTERNS IN THE SKY

Whimpering repeatedly
Is this how I've spent my time?
A lantern stands appealingly
It has just entered its prime

Our paranoid memories
Have brought me here
Into the sky I release
My hope and fear

Forgiveness is a lantern
Concealing my passive anger
Dismissing it is not my concern
My doubts began to harbour

Thousands of golden shells
Brighten the seemingly non-polluted sky
Ringing in me are bells
Seeing them go infinitely high

In the galaxy spirits embark
My hands feel empty for now
Eyes search in the dark
As the lanterns return somehow

The sky gives the lanterns a shove
They're bound to come back to me
People pass by without even looking above
It's necessary

They have to float under their own power
Waiting for one to be destroyed
Or they stay airborne forever
Can the sky be void?

Stiff edge, rigid mind add on
Burdensome to watch it burst
Don't try to find it, it's gone
I've to prepare the next like the first

Erasing time is what I try to do
Your existence is not to be criticised
One achievement is what it comes down to
The lanterns need to disappear or be minimised

DREAMS IN AN AIRCRAFT

A long flight
Led to the rise of a conundrum
Trembling height
Wasn't any more troublesome

Among the crying babies
And the noisy passengers
I lost the little fees
To support my secretive majors

My naive heart wished upon a thorn
Up and down went the plane
My fear was reborn
As I buckled the seat belt with pain

A sigh of relief!
As thoughts keep jouncing
They tried to stay brief
Like the hostess announcing

A true delicacy served
Killed the hot passion I had
Filled my stomach that starved
A few attempts don't let it go bad

My dreams are vivid
I made them that way
The airplane didn't skid
While it landed on the same day

Unloading the luggage
My efforts are unseen
Stuck in the zone amongst the rage
Towards the exit, others lean

What I flee
Were my hopes to be the best
Which seemed to bind me
In the "survival of the fittest"

THE BRIDE OF 1947

"What's gifted isn't meant to be returned"
She was taught while grooming
This lesson is to be learned
By every flower that is blooming

She followed what was said
As she arrived years later
To see a empty house ahead
Left behind by her mater

A dusty room making her feet black
Had sold for a reasonable price
She took some stuff to pack
And locked the room in a trice

She no longer rests
In the arms of her origin
She is merely one of the guests
Whose familiarity lies in the bin

They played with dolls together
One of them was much prettier
She kept wondering whether
Beauty is a subjective peer

While she was looking at her watch
A little hand tapped on her back
Asking her to play Hopscotch
For which she had a knack

Lightly jumping to a square
Her steps get heavy
Tricks lie bare
So the children set her free

Blood runs thicker than water
An ill-effect of affection
Like an unskilled potter
She created this defection

Misconceptions protected her
From the bullets of the society
She wanted to change the future
But got stuck in the harsh reality

A bond of sacrifice
Connected their heart
But a needless advice
Drove them apart

Her dear heart possesses
Some amiable instances
And a few old dresses
She wears according to conveniences

SOCIALIZING

A group of people
Passing by my house
Which was once very quiet
And had only my spouse

They sing and dance
The same way every year
We watch like we've never before
But don't go any near

The energy they pour out
Is absorbed by us
Unknowingly going along
As we see all the fuss

They consider it a festivity
To celebrate something holy
Releasing our elation in captivity
Into the crowded sea

Smiles and sweets

Consumed by our lips

Good fellowship completes

The exchanged tips

Mere inclusion

Did our home environment well

Enjoying with strangers in profusion

Let us come out of the shell

Keya Jadhav

BALLERINA

A ballerina with grace
Is a treat to everyone's eyes
Not a word out of her mouth
She never cuts her ties

Rotating on the metal cylinder
To prepare our vision with pink
An aesthetic effect
Into the heart it doesn't sink

When hurdles won't let her balance
Unprofessional for us to fix
Dear oh dear! She tells us
As we try to get near her and mix

Going back to what she does
As little kids begin to disperse
Performing round the clock
Avoiding the need to rehearse

Her attention meets mine
With avoidable fondness
Others turn a blind eye
While she kindles our closeness

A music box
To see her occasionally
Which is never opened
Till the glitter gets sully

Designed to display tenderness
We take her for granted
Her box never shuts us out
Many connections it bred

I will turn like her one day
Sharing a similar story
The unspoken words between us
Will restore the former glory

A TALE OF TWO MEN

Two very tired men
Sought shelter in a cabin
A wizard lived there
Who even served them gin

After a drink or two
The wizard got tipsy
And revealed all his secrets
That made the men go hehe

Then he indicated a treasure
Only to be found deep in a cave
And to reach there he had a map
Which he handed to Dave

No one has succeeded
In finding a jewel so rare
And if someone came close
They could only stare

It intrigued their minds
And made them wonder
What kind of a beauty it was
And how it continued to prosper

Thus began a journey
Across mountains and seas
Dave and Josh rode a horse
Which they got on a lease

"Our troubles will leave us behind"
"Once we reach there to find"
Their quest to conquer the treasure
Spoke of their innocent mind

Rocky roads tested their patience
Well, the journey's only begun
"You're the one to blame!"
Is what took out all the fun

They shared the seat to heaven
A competition drove their ride
Helping each other upfront
So their greed can hide

On the night of the full moon
The three stopped to rest
A loud noise startled them
It was storm: the uninvited guest

"Oh freak! We won't survive now"
Josh exclaimed trembling head to toe
Started a prayer to strike a deal with god
At the cost of a sacrifice, is what the horse didn't know

So the bearer of death
Even made the animal repent
A nice little kick
Was the horse's goodbye present

Shrugging their shoulders
They called its disappearance a mystique
Moving ahead with the sunrise
They heard neighs all week

Marching like soldiers in a parade
Their pride overtaking speed
The birds on trees laughed
At the leisurely walk indeed

Reaching where they should
With the soles of the shoes worn out
Lied ahead a no man's land
Dave almost blacked out

"Where are the precious rubies?"
"Oh! Where is the gold chest?"
Words mixed up the expectation of 'magnificent'
Because there was only a mermaid sitting on a crest

The low lying hill lured them towards itself
The figuration of the enchantress made them surprised
After all they made it this far
Too see the charms of the femme fatal unsupervised

With a few closer looks
Dave and Josh dropped down on their knees
"You shall be my lady"
Said each, seeing an opportunity to seize

The mermaid too
Wasn't as down to earth as she seemed
For there was duel she recommended
It accidentally got their ancestors redeemed

Swords were thrown around
To create a legacy
Their huge-belly elders
Did nothing but pass on a egoistic spree

Josh stabbed Dave
A moment of silence
Could he have stayed with the mermaid?
At avoidable violence

"He'll meet pretty charmers in heaven" thought Josh
Unaware of the consequences of their actions
Dave was halfway to hell
Where he gave feet messages to ogresses in dungeons

Josh lived this experience on earth
At the feet of a pretty woman
The wizard became wise to him
For warning them to run

Almost spend an eternity on that land
She asked for pearls by the bay
He once told her to dive into the ocean and get it herself
He has never been seen since that day

Sitting on the rock peacefully
She saw two new men approaching
Fighting to win her over
Josh and Dave enjoyed the poaching

BRIM

Others collections brought their way
Into my empty jar with handful marbles
Played along and filled it to its brim
Spectrum of colours shone like a glim

I competed to fill as I had to
Why does this incompetence seem trivial?
I could place those glass rocks anywhere
And still have admirers not mind the fare

Decorating the never-changing transparency
They are becoming forgetful of their purpose
I can handle losing them with criticism
Than live with broken pieces of prism

The marbles have been passed down since generations
Buying new ones were a luxury
We have evolved every decade
Bringing our own will encourage their trade

A set of unseen marbles
Is what fascinates me every time
Winning according to the prize
Will keep me interested and wise

Keya Jadhav

LOWER HOUSE

A flight of paper stairs
Led to a lavish penthouse
A place that existed only in my wishful dreams
Whose flames I'd occasionally douse

Everyday I'd climb that spiral concrete
Never even glanced at the elevator
Always bending my knees to move forward
So my sustainer doesn't call me a traitor

Servers ran around
To bring everything to me
In the house I bought
I don't know where the salt cellar can be

My workers talk among themselves
Little to do with what I think
Talking about the movie playing in the theatre
Or their young girls wearing dresses of glittery pink

Stayed away for an overnight project
We had dinner and wine to prep
Arriving home late night
Sweet silence welcomed me at the doorstep

The house lit up in the moonlight
Screaming tiredness tiptoed across the wooden floor
I spent a sleepless night
Thinking of times spent ashore

The next day I was running towards the ocean
Wet sand ingrained in the empty lines of my feet
Unlike the lines of destiny in my palm
Which my future declared obsolete

Like a child fascinated by the currents of the blue
Back and forth, I filled the house with sticky rubbles of land
Drowned my innocence in a pool of age
While standing on the tidal-home bearing creation of sand

Calm adventures end quickly
At a snap of the finger, the humidity disappeared
Mundane activities repeated
Till my inner peace feared

Hiking the delicate steps to the pinnacle of my bed
Benjamin Franklin* never looked more proud
Always exposed to the risk of crumbling
I never made my opinions loud

Took off my socks and laid back on the couch
My reality lies outside the water bubble
Despite the transparency
The joyful limitations make me stumble

*Benjamin Franklin appears on the $100 bill

FEW MORE MINUTES OF SLEEP

The wet misty cars welcome the morning rain, while I lie half-awake in my bed. Cosy under the blanket of responsibilities, the warmth pacifies my arduous feet.

A tender body lies on the mattress, a motionless corporeal of past.

The melodious chirping is my alarm, to incarnate into a world of fresh chaos. I'm well aware of how my day starts, yet I want to take a step back.

Resume in the hour of the inexperienced, with hazy surroundings, when I can sense through my blind-spot a perfect place.

A commune of lush kids, running in circle of a garden. I want to hold their plump hands, and contrast my high strength as they invite me with a shy smile. And when I see them wiping the salty drops near their mouth, I jump into a wagon.

I drive to the farthest corner the fuel can take me.

And if I run out…………..I will run out.

CAUGHT IN A STORM

Running down the narrow path
She burst the door open
Dripping from head to toe
Appeared a upset nun

Furious and Bored
Zeus brought terror upon the town
Failure to escape it
Made her loyalty frown

A young girl with red cheeks
Confined her childhood for a shield
Desperately holding onto innocence
Time has become a transcendent yield

Church, a new purpose
Church, a new home
Church, a new world
Church, a new Rome

The mortal being on the cross
Empowers her with vigour
Smiling upon her suffering
Together they've crossed the Jordon River

Devotion lies in her thoughts
Praying everyday won't bring salvation
Not like undertaking a task
Sunday service should be a vacation

Beginning to live with mistakes
She's recreating her existence
Happiness spurs from her heart
As little steps fill her dance

Complimenting her compassionate nature
A traditional routine still rests in her memory
With a fiancé by her side
She looks up to Jesus and Mary

THE DAY A CHILD WAS BORN

Under the snow white light, cries a new born dwarf

The first one in the forest of creatures

With his white robe hanging loosely on his hands

And the mellow rain running down his red cheeks

Oh, you with invisible eyelids. Will you stay that way forever?

He carries a blunt axe

To collect pieces of wood from chopped trees

Trying to build a house of those

Instead of a fire to keep him warm

He acquired a cottage with a big table

To serve a stomach filled with herb soup

Couldn't find any chocolates

The sweet words would melt in his mouth

The leftovers of nature

Fed his heart with six others delicacies

And the currents of the river

Made satiety return for more

The muddy trail erases his footprints as they grow

So he marches with all his might

A glorious imprint of the gone

Sits on a majestic throne in his mind

Looking through the deep mirror

Only fishes and gas bubbles reflect his truth

A tale that has given him a gasp of curiosity

Swims in circles of conviction

A smiling child, who is seeing the world through his glasses

A broken piece from a crack endangers his direction

Pray your fate doesn't entangle with that of the princess

OH, MY LOVELY SWAN

A swan dressed in silk

Behind the translucent sheets of haven

Peeks through her black rosy eyes

Into the shadows of Cobs* delicately engraven

As the frigid fog welcomes the sunrise

She warms the cushion meekly

Moving swiftly like a cherry blossom petal

When water ripples under the moonlight weakly

Singing in a voice dripping nasality

She fills the gathering with an aroma

Alluring the tea-cups of Dannas*

Towards the beak from Oklahoma

Face as white as sake*

Conceals expressions that look gushy

Gliding across the lake in a flash

She comes forth with flawless Kanzashi*

Half-drawn drapes remain unobtrusive
Kaleidoscopic birds spin a serene world
Dried tears displaying the belle of feathers
Encounter ears that are truly pearled

Feet that move inches apart
Have sheltered in a lifelong manoeuvre
Wrapped in crimson, a tender youth
Feasts artistically on a Louvar

* Cobs - male swan
  Danna - a wealthy client
  Sake - rice wine
  Kanzashi - hair ornament

Shove the rocks aside

Midst the chatter of thin hands

To make room for brood

岩を脇に押し出す

細い手のおしゃべりの真っ只中

ひなのためのスペースを作るために

A bovine schedule:
Amble across busy roads
Still chewing on grass

牛のスケジュール：
混雑した道路を横切ってアンブル
まだ草を噛んでいる

Keya Jadhav

February
S M T W T F S
1 2 3 4 5 6
7 8 9 10 11 12 13
14 15 16 17 18 19 20
21 22 23 24 25 26 27
28

A 7-DAY LIFE

Laziness causing delay
For a day's worth of pay
From myself, I'm led astray
By the spiteful Monday

Feeling less grey
On my bed, I stay
Work piled up like hay
On the usual Tuesday

Mind like a rustic bouquet
In the mid-week of disarray
Moulding plans like clay
During the impatient Wednesday

Pleasure is underway
Delightful meal becomes a prey
Nothing much to say
On the peaceful Thursday

Smiling upon a clique:
How light my duties weigh
Ignored advices bring may
To the jovial Friday

Spending time by the bay
From the city, I'm far away
In the pleasant breeze I play
On the soothing Saturday

Talking to my mates in the cafe
A warm fellowship they portray
All these moments I replay
While going to bed on Sunday

Keya Jadhav

A PRINTER

Printing documents about tax
The cartridge is wearing itself out
A chance to express its own perspective
Turns into endless doubt

Every few hours a command is given
And to follow is to survive
Years of habit comes in hand
With the documents considered naive

But on one day out of seven
It exists as a time traveller
Through its button pupils
The fading colour becomes a story teller

The still pictures of employees
Bring out delightful memories
When they take small breaks
To finish their long stories

As their lungs are filled
With the scent of ink papers
Huge mugs of coffee turn
The tired auras into vapours

Images of the whispered jokes
And their talks in the cubicle
Between office hours
Their stress is declared null

From the early morning yawns
To the company dinners late night
A utopian room in a commercial building
Is created by a big machine in sight

Like a black cat crossing the road
It exists in a disguise
Hoping to change its environment
For the gullible flies

The printing cycle of whoosh
Comes to a stop when the moon comes out
It spent its day softening observations
And returns to its original route

DIETES BICOLOR

Faint neon flowers
From a shady growth
Purple and orange
You dismiss both

Long green leaves
Reflecting its true nature
Never seen anyone
With such high stature

Unable to explore
It's frightful freshness
With its smooth petals
To maintain its wellness

Spots of purple
Too many to count
When accompanied by
Undisturbed clumps in large amount

Its florescence is

Holding up with the drought

All I can remember is

What this fortnight lily brought

Keya Jadhav

PAID LEAVE

Over the fence on a paid leave

Bolts a quirky refugee

Well frogs jump behind me

Don't scare me, just take a leap of faith

Let's sail through the seven continents

And stumble upon a Santa María

Only clothes dance on the reflecting peninsula

On the melody of the restless guitar

Any time of the day carries the same plane

To decorate the fool's paradise

An envelope carrying the texture of an old paper

Welcomes steady fingers for a quill

Camping in December at the dead of night

Allows the brightest fire to melt the snow

The pale yellow pee of a newborn

Is more cherished than gold

A tinkering shade makes it heavier

The strain in your talk is easy to detect

Like the radio frequency waves

The oddly fitting verbs are a futile ignorance

For a life-sentencing abyss

EARTHEN POT

Living my life is like winning an Oscar

Sitting among the beautiful faces of art

If you are one of the few

Who could lay hands on undefined assent

Then your life is in hope for the rigid figure

A pursuit of being declared the finest

You're an earthen pot in a chamber of clay

If you just step around the thousand chairs

And pull down the dreamy dress of daze

The toes might sensitize the heels that waft on stilettos

Yet anonymous glimmers in the spotlight

At the celebration of a filled vessel

Moustaches and masks can hide

The cat-eyes and whiskers of aesthetic

To bring them a persisting idol

And closing the curtains on it

FOOTPRINTS ON THE PALACE LINOLEUM

Can I lift the wavering flag stationed on the podium?

The chronicle of faces awaited my intention in hysterics

Time turns countless Charles' into relics

While watching over the barricades of folium

We persevered while marching on hymns of the harmonium

To intercept with the obligation of armed generics

But I deciphered the fallen stars in their ageless spherics

Which prompted me to place new footprints on the palace linoleum

A ringmaster can pose as the teacher of claps

Gathering his fête will only continue for a span

Clawing at him, the tricolour flaps

Sending the red cap across miles of forests to every man

So they can join me in the city that slaps

For I looked through my binoculars to be called Marianne

- Inspired by "La Liberté guidant le people" by Eugène Delacroix

9 789354 587702